Grammar Ray

Please return on or before the latest date above.
You can renew online at www.kent.gov.uk/libs
or by phone 08458 247 200

rammar

andrew carter

Published by Evans Brothers Limited
2A Portman Mansions
Chiltern Street
London W1U 6NR

© in this edition Evans Brothers Limited 2010
© in the text and illustrations Andrew Carter 2010

Printed in Malta by Gutenberg Press

Editor: Nicola Edwards
Designer: Mark Holt

British Library Cataloguing in Publication Data

Carter, Andrew.
Verbs. — (Grammar Ray)
1. English language—Verb—Juvenile literature.
I. Title II. Series
425.6-dc22

ISBN-13: 9780237538484

contents

INTRODUCTION

Hello and welcome to Grammar Ray! You are about to enter a world of fun and adventure, where English grammar is brought to life. Words in the English language can be divided into different groups called 'parts of speech'. In this title, we will join the robots in their quest to explore the role of the verb.

I'm the mighty Verb-Man. Stick with me and I'll show you how to travel through time.

The first part of the book is a comic strip. Join Verb-Man as he battles against a metallic menace from the future and travels backwards and forwards in time, using the power of verbs to help him. Look out for the words in green - they are key.

After you've seen Verb-Man's adventures, the rest of the book looks at verbs in more detail, and gives some more examples. Use this if you need a reminder of the role verbs play in English grammar. It also requires your puzzle-solving skills and tests what you have learnt along the way. So be sure to pay attention!

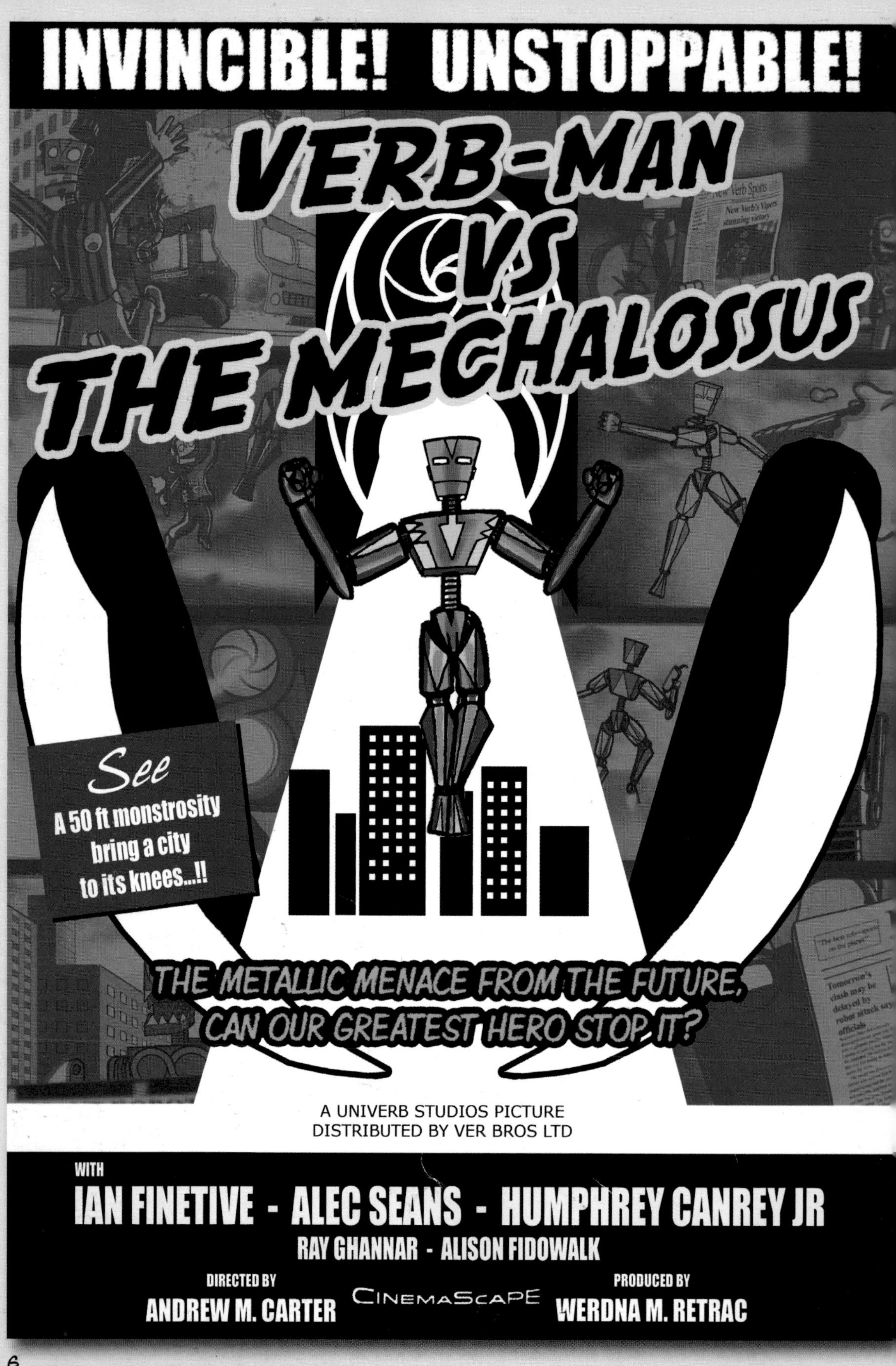

INVINCIBLE! UNSTOPPABLE!
VERB-MAN VS THE MECHALOSSUS
New Verb Sports
New Verb's Vipers stunning victory
See
A 50 ft monstrosity bring a city to its knees...!!
THE METALLIC MENACE FROM THE FUTURE, CAN OUR GREATEST HERO STOP IT?
A UNIVERB STUDIOS PICTURE
DISTRIBUTED BY VER BROS LTD
WITH
IAN FINETIVE - ALEC SEANS - HUMPHREY CANREY JR
RAY GHANNAR - ALISON FIDOWALK
DIRECTED BY
ANDREW M. CARTER
CINEMASCAPE
PRODUCED BY
WERDNA M. RETRAC

►PLAY

UNI**V**ERB

STUDIOS PRESENTS

VERB-MAN
VS
THE MECHALOSSUS

New Verb City - Morning

Neko

New Verb Sports

New Verb's Vipers
stunning victory

PAUSE

We can think of verbs as ACTION WORDS.

PLAY

To fly,

to shoot,

to lift,

to explode.*

BOOM!!

*The form of a verb preceded by 'to' is known as the *infinitive*.

Some verbs describe other ways in which people behave:

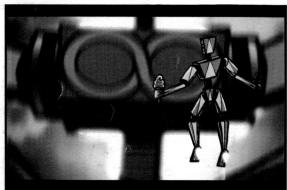

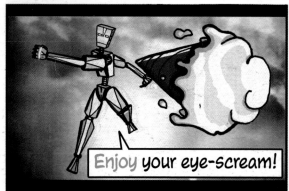

DISTRIBUTED BY UNIVERB STUDIOS AND VER BROS LTD

MONSTROUS! TERRIFYING!

VERB-MAN AND THE TERROR FROM TIME

A UNIVERB STUDIOS PICTURE

DISTRIBUTED BY VER BROS LTD

See
A horror from the depths of history!

IAN FINETIVE - MARY OTHAR - PETER ROFESA

DIRECTED BY
ANDREW M. CARTER

CinemaScape

PRODUCED BY
WERDNA M. RETRAC

▶PLAY

UNIVERB

STUDIOS PRESENTS

VERB-MAN AND THE TERROR FROM TIME

New Verb City Museum

Grand Museum Opening

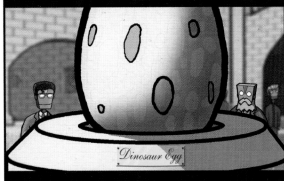

Dinosaur Egg

Professor, where did you find all these fantastic exhibits?

Private

Well, Vincent, let me show you.

My time machine.

❙❙ PAUSE

Verbs can be used to tell us when something took place.

For example, to describe what happened in the PAST.

PLAY

With my machine I travelled back in time...

ONE YEAR EARLIER

I collected many rare objects.

It was in prehistory that I found my greatest treasure...

ROAAR!!

PAUSE

Verbs are also used to tell us when something is happening in the PRESENT. For example...

PLAY

CRACK CRACK

What is that cracking noise I can hear?

CRACK

CRACK CRACK CRACK CRACK

The egg is hatching!

14

RA RA!

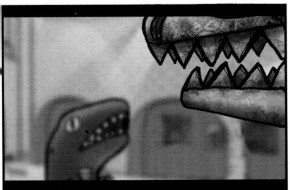

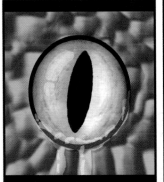

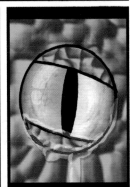

RAAAA!!

Where did you go, Vincent?

Someone must stop that monster!

Look, Verb-Man is here!

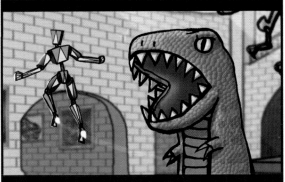

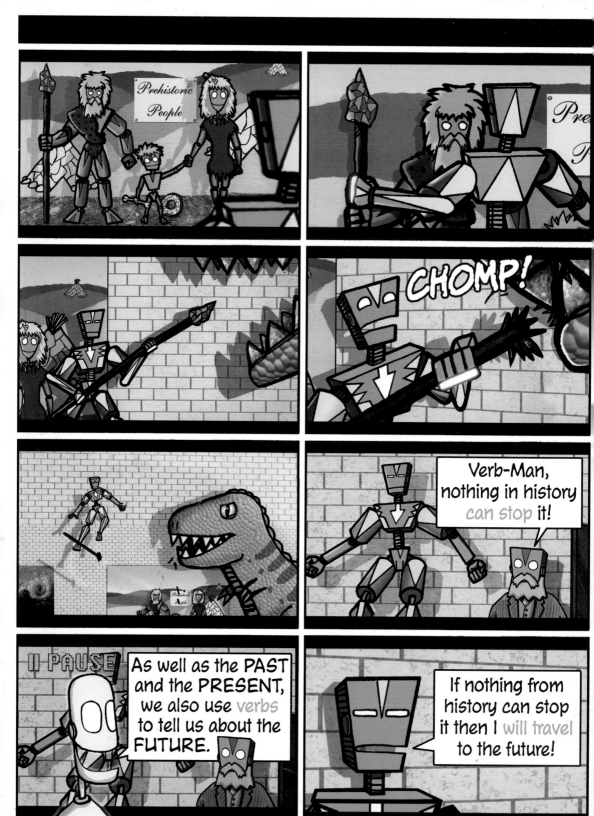

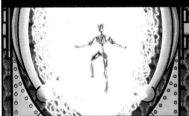
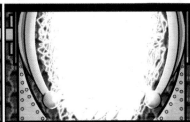

It is going to eat me and my baby!

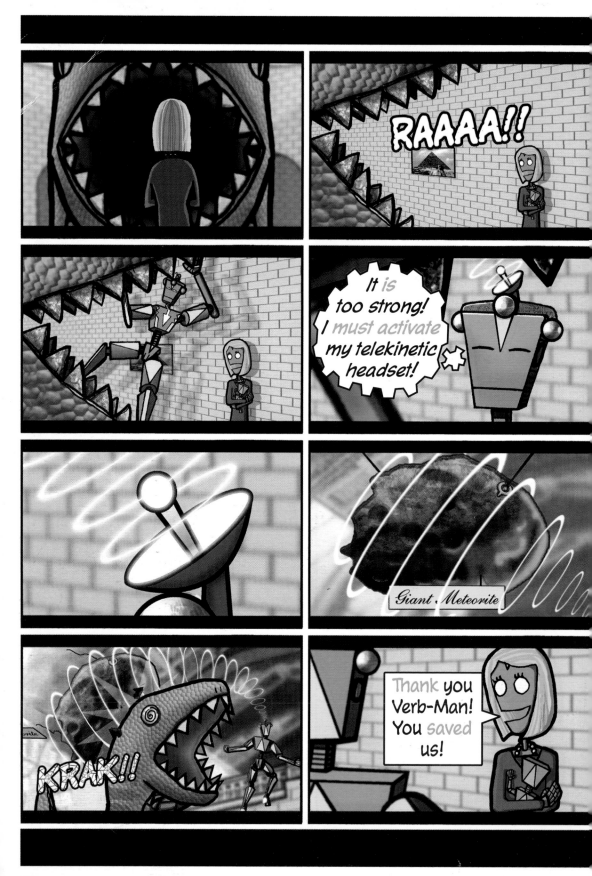

65,000,000 years earlier

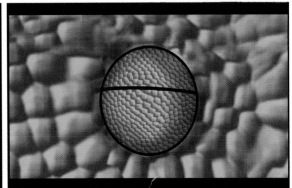

more about verbs

verbs

Verbs are very important – every sentence contains a verb. A verb is commonly called a 'doing' word. It can tell us about a physical or mental action. Sometimes the action isn't all that obvious, and refers to a state of being.

FOR EXAMPLE:

PHYSICAL ACTIONS — *to jump, to play, to swim*

MENTAL ACTIONS — *to dream, to consider, to wonder*

A STATE OF BEING — *to be, to exist*

NOTE:

The infinitive is the basic form of the verb. It is usually preceded by *'to'*.

Tenses

We use verb tenses to tell us <u>when</u> something happens.
There are three main tenses.

PRESENT TENSE

The present tense is used to describe actions that are happening now. We can use it in three different ways.

The *Present Simple* is used for things that are always true or for regular events.

FOR EXAMPLE:

The sun <u>shines</u> in the morning.
I <u>feed</u> my pet shark every day.

The *Present Continuous* describes an action that is happening right now.

FOR EXAMPLE:

I <u>am reading</u> an interesting book.
She <u>is thinking</u> about rabbits.

The *Present Perfect* can tell us about the present and past at the same time.

FOR EXAMPLE:

I <u>have played</u> tennis since last year = I started playing tennis last year and I still play.

PAST TENSE

The past tense describes things that have already happened, that are in the past. There are different types of past tense, but the two simplest and most common are:

The *Past Simple*, which is used for a single event that happened in the past and is finished or complete.

FOR EXAMPLE:

Yesterday I <u>saw</u> a dolphin.
Last week Verb-Man <u>rescued</u> a robot.

The *Past Simple* is different from the *Present Perfect*, described on page 20, because it tells us about an action that has ended.

FOR EXAMPLE:

I <u>lived</u> in the jungle for two years = I lived in the jungle in the past but I don't live there any more.

The *Present Perfect*, on the other hand, tells us about an event that began in the past but that is still continuing.

FOR EXAMPLE:

I <u>have lived</u> in the jungle for two years = I lived in the jungle for two years and I am still living there.

Another common type of past tense is the *Past Continuous*. This can be used to describe an action in the past that was interrupted by another event.

FOR EXAMPLE:

Yesterday, while I <u>was looking</u> at the ocean, I saw a dolphin.
Last week, while he <u>was fighting</u> a robot, Verb-Man rescued a young boy.

FUTURE TENSE

The future tense talks about things that are going to happen. There are two common ways to talk about the future: *will* and *going to*.

FOR EXAMPLE:

I <u>will</u> have a hamburger and a salad please.
I'm <u>going to</u> go to Mars for my holiday this summer.

Regular and irregular verbs

Verbs can be split up into regular and irregular verbs.

REGULAR VERBS   Regular verbs always behave in the same way in the different tenses.

FOR EXAMPLE:	PRESENT TENSE	PAST TENSE	PRESENT PERFECT TENSE
	I wonder	*I wondered*	*I have wondered*
	You watch	*You watched*	*You have watched*
	He plays	*He played*	*He has played*
	We are walking	*We walked*	*We have walked*
	They jump	*They jumped*	*They have jumped*

IRREGULAR VERBS   These are verbs that do not follow the regular pattern. Instead of adding an *–ed* to the end to create the past tense, the verb itself changes. You can find out how each irregular verb changes in different tenses by looking it up in a dictionary.

FOR EXAMPLE:	PRESENT TENSE	PAST TENSE	PRESENT PERFECT TENSE
	I swim	*I swam*	*I have swum*
	You sing	*You sang*	*You have sung*
	She is drinking	*She drank*	*She has drunk*
	We feel	*We felt*	*We have felt*
	They are catching	*They caught*	*They have caught*

verbs
test yourself

1. Which of the following is a verb?

(a) Shark   (b) Dangerous   (c) Swim   (d) Hungrily

2. In the following sentences, do the underlined verbs refer to:
the past,   the present,   the past and the present,   the future?

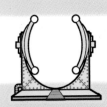  

(a) Verb-Man <u>will fight</u> evil whenever it arises.
(b) The professor <u>is wearing</u> a time-belt.
(c) The time-machine <u>was constructed</u> inside the museum.
(d) Verb-Man <u>has been protecting</u> New Verb City for many years.

3. Are the following verbs regular or irregular?
(a) fly   (b) open   (c) like   (d) think   (e) play

Turn the page upside-down to see the answers!